Praise
Economics

"It is a terrific book that covers the basic ideas of economics in a compelling way for elementary and middle school students."

- Jere R. Behrman, William R. Kenan, Jr.
Professor of Economics, University of Pennsylvania

• •

"This is an excellent introduction to economics for young readers that cultivates economic intuition and motivates students to apply economic principles in daily lives."

- Economics Alum, Harvard University

Table of Contents

Chapter 1: The Basics

Chapter 2: Market Systems and Economies

Chapter 3: Money

Chapter 4: The US Economy

Chapter 5: Gross Domestic Product

Chapter 6: Basic Business Concepts

Chapter 7: International Trade

An Introductory Page

Before we dive into the book, let's learn about goods and services!

Goods

Goods are tangible items that satisfy consumer wants. Consumer goods include things like bagels, textbooks, and laptops.

Services

Services are non-tangible actions that satisfy consumer wants. Services include providing haircuts, medical examinations, and education to consumers.

Chapter 1: The Basics

- 1.1 Scarcity and Choices
- 1.2 Supply and Demand
- 1.3 Marginal Analysis
- 1.4 Production Possibilities
- What is Economics?

Hello! My name is Orpple. I will be accompanying you on your journey through the world of economics! Whether you know it or not, economics is a big part of our daily lives. For example, we are always faced with choices. Just this morning, I had to decide whether I wanted pancakes or a muffin for breakfast. this is the idea of scarcity and choice.

1

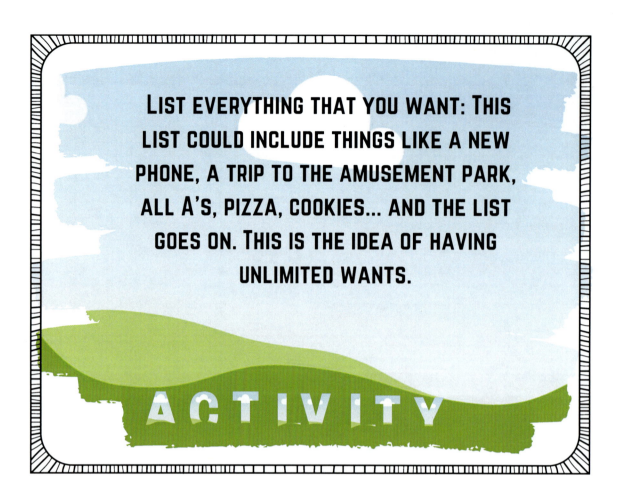

LIST EVERYTHING THAT YOU WANT: THIS LIST COULD INCLUDE THINGS LIKE A NEW PHONE, A TRIP TO THE AMUSEMENT PARK, ALL A'S, PIZZA, COOKIES... AND THE LIST GOES ON. THIS IS THE IDEA OF HAVING UNLIMITED WANTS.

ACTIVITY

1.1 Scarcity and Choices

Types of Resources

In economics, there are four types of resources: land, labor, capital, and entrepreneurship.

- **Land**: Land includes all natural resources such as water, trees, and soil. Water can be used for many household, industrial, and environmental activities. For example, think about the water you use to brush your teeth, to generate electricity, and to water grass.
- **Labor**: Labor includes the workers that are needed to produce goods and services. The desk and chair you

are working on right now were created by designers and builders who provided their labor.

- **Capital**: Capital includes the machinery that is needed to produce goods and services. This textbook was printed using a printing machine. The printing machine is capital. Other examples of capital include tractors, laptops, and factory buildings.
- **Entrepreneurship**: The person who puts land, labor, and capital to use is known as an entrepreneur. Entrepreneurs take risks that combine the previous three resources: land, labor, and capital.

The Idea of Limited Resources

All valued resources are limited! For example, think of the lined paper in your binder. Once you use them all, you will not have any paper left. This means that lined paper is a **limited resource**.

Additionally, on farms, trees are cut down to make paper. If too many trees are cut down, then there would not be enough trees to produce paper. Therefore, trees are another example of a limited resource.

If only the trees around me are unlimited!

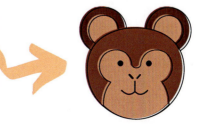

Chapter 1 the Basics

Having to make a Choice

Now that you have learned about the idea of scarcity and limited resources, you understand why we have to make choices. Our wants are unlimited, but resources are limited. This means that we cannot have everything we want and we have to make choices.

1.2 Supply and Demand

Who are demanders and suppliers?

Buyers are the consumers of goods and services, and thus they create demand. **Demand** is created when a consumer is able and willing to buy a certain good at set prices, assuming all other factors are held constant (ceteris paribus). When you go shopping with your parents and you want and are financially able to buy a pair of jeans, you are creating demand! However, even if you really want those jeans, but are not able to afford them, you are not actually demanding that good.

Quantity demanded is the amount of a good or service that the consumer is willing and able to purchase at a certain price. Each combination of price and the quantity demanded comes together to create the entire demand curve, which is downward sloping and shows an inverse relationship between price and the quantity demanded. Think about it - when the price goes up, there will be less quantity demanded, because fewer consumers would be willing and able to purchase the goods or services at a higher price. On the contrary, when price goes down, quantity demanded will increase, due to the increased number of consumers that are willing and able to purchase the goods or services.

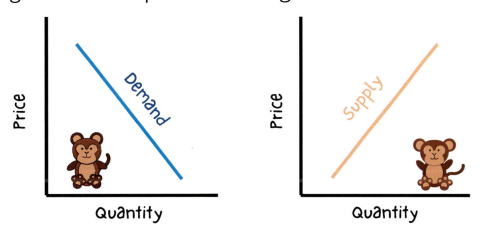

The other side of the market is supply. **Supply** is the amount of a good or service that producers are willing and able to sell at set prices, ceteris paribus.

Quantity supplied is the amount of a good or service that the producer is willing and able to sell at a certain price. The combinations of price and quantity supplied create the supply curve, which is upward sloping and shows a direct relationship between price and the quantity supplied. On the supply side, when price goes up, quantity supplied will increase, because producers will have chances of increased profits, leading to them being willing and able to sell more of their product. However, when price decreases, quantity supplied will also decrease (producers are less willing and able to sell their products).

5

The Equilibrium Point

You may be wondering, how are prices and quantities set in the market? Well, it all comes down to the interaction of the supply and demand curves. These curves intersect at the **equilibrium point**, where quantity supplied is exactly equal to quantity demanded! The price and quantity are then set at their intersection point (shown on graph below). Together, demand and supply truly create the basis of the market system.

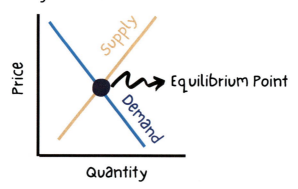

1.3 Marginal Analysis

When you are having a pizza party, how do you decide whether you want that extra slice of pizza that just looks so tempting? When you have three exams the next day, which one do you spend more time studying for? Or even better, would you eat 5 red velvet cupcakes and 6 muffins, or 6 red velvet cupcakes and 5 muffins? Congratulations, you just engaged in marginal analysis thinking!

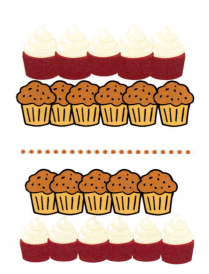

Marginal analysis is an important tool when making decisions, especially when thinking at the margin, by examining the additional (marginal) benefits derived from something as compared to the additional (marginal) costs incurred. As learned previously, all resources are scarce, and marginal analysis helps us make the best choices on where to allocate those scarce resources in order to gain as much benefit as possible while minimizing the costs.

It is always logical to do something (such as eating cake, finding the "right" amount of pollution, and studying for an exam) when the marginal cost of doing so is equal to the marginal benefit. This way, our marginal benefit would be maximized! If the marginal cost of doing something is greater than the marginal benefit, it is not reasonable to continue doing the activity, because your benefit is less than the costs. Similarly, if the marginal benefit is greater than the marginal cost, then it means that we are not getting enough of this good / activity / service, because we would gain even more benefit by having more. In economics, benefits should always be maximized.

Marginal Cost < Marginal Benefit

Marginal Cost = Marginal Benefit

Marginal Cost > Marginal Benefit

1.4 Production Possibilities

Let's pretend for a second that you live in a country called Econville that only produces two goods: oil and strawberries.

However, there is only a limited amount of resources that the country has, and therefore must allocate the resources between producing oil and strawberries. To illustrate this idea, there is the **production possibilities curve**, or PPC (also known as the production possibilities frontier). The PPC shows all of the possible combinations of two goods (in this case, oil and strawberries) that can be produced with the limited amount of resources and technology that Econville has.

Every single point either on the curve (efficient) or below the curve (underutilized resources) is a possible combination that Econville could produce for oil and strawberries. The combinations that are on the curve are efficient whereas the combinations below the curve are inefficient because resources are being underutilized. In this case, the curve isn't linear - it's bowed out. Why? As we produce increasingly more of one good, we are giving up the other good in greater amounts. This is because not all of the resources that Econville has are equally suited toward producing oil and strawberries. When Econville first allocates some resources toward strawberries, they only give up a little of oil, because they are first using the land that is great for producing strawberries, but terrible for oil. However, as they keep allocating more and more resources toward strawberries, they give up more oil, because the land that they are using to produce strawberries is not as great for producing the fruit as when they only produced a little.

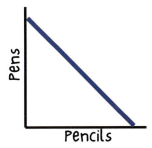

Now, let's assume that another country, Microville, produces only two goods: pens and pencils. Since the resources for producing these two goods are very similar, the PPC would be linear, meaning that as they produce more pens, they give up constant amounts of pencils.

The PPC, no matter what shape, illustrates the idea of **trade-offs**: we will always have to give up some of one good in order to receive more of another good.

Underutilization

Well, what happens if the countries don't produce a combination of the two goods that is on the curve? What if they produce inside the curve? This shows an **underutilization** of resources. Given their current technology and resources, the countries would not be producing at their full potential.

Unattainable Production

Points beyond the PPC are impossible to reach. This is because there are simply not enough resources to produce the certain combination of goods.

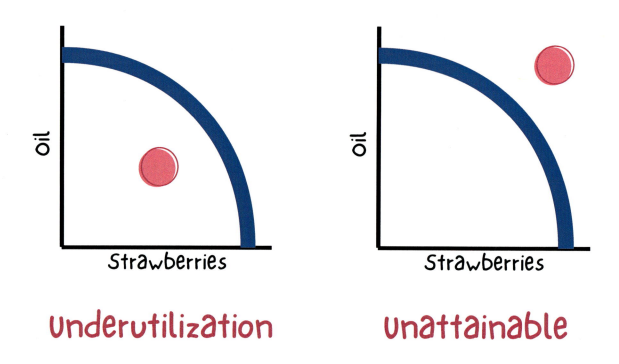

What is Economics?

Now that you've dipped your toes into the world of Economics... what exactly is it?

Economics

is the study of

SCARCITY

and

CHOICE

Chapter 2: Market Systems and Economies

- 2.1 What is a Market?
- 2.2 Free Market System
- 2.3 Market Structures
- 2.4 Types of Economies
- Countries on the Economic Spectrum

2.1 What is a Market?

A **market** is a place where people can exchange goods and services. Your local grocery store, a local factory, and a local recreation center are all examples of markets. At a grocery store, food is exchanged for money. At a local factory, workers exchange their labor for wages. At a recreation center, money is exchanged for leisure. Markets are everywhere in our daily lives!

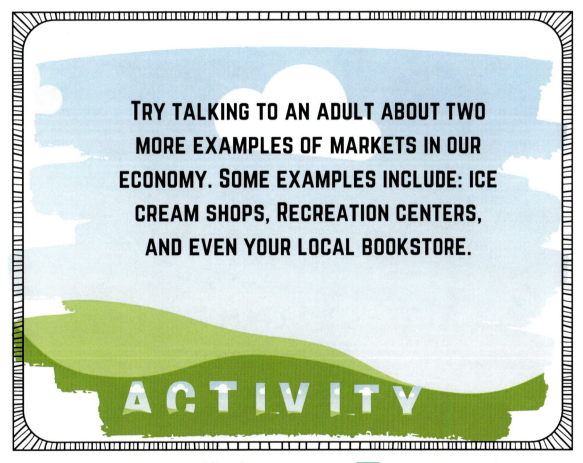

TRY TALKING TO AN ADULT ABOUT TWO MORE EXAMPLES OF MARKETS IN OUR ECONOMY. SOME EXAMPLES INCLUDE: ICE CREAM SHOPS, RECREATION CENTERS, AND EVEN YOUR LOCAL BOOKSTORE.

ACTIVITY

Chapter 2 Market Systems and Economies

2.2 The Free Market System

You have the freedom to buy a house, eat cookies, and choose what color to paint your room. You have the freedom to decide what to do, and what not to do, without excessive government control over your actions. Essentially, you have the right to make decisions for yourself. The basis of the free market system is supply and demand (do you see how everything is starting to tie together?)

2.3 Market Structures

There are four main types of markets that appear in our global economy.

The four different market structures are:
- Perfect Competition
- Monopolistic Competition
- Oligopoly
- Monopoly

Perfect Competition

In a **perfectly competitive market**, businesses all sell the exact same good at the exact same price. One example of perfect competition is agriculture.

Think of your favorite fruit or vegetable! Most grocery stores will sell your favorite fruit or vegetable at the same price: the market price. In a perfectly competitive market, the market price is the same as the equilibrium price. The forces of supply and demand determine the market price.

Monopolistic Competition

In a **monopolistic competitive market**, there are many businesses that sell differentiated products. This means that the businesses in monopolistic competition do not sell the exact same product as the other businesses. Having a slight difference in their products allows them to have some control over their price. Examples of businesses in monopolistic competition include restaurants and retail stores. Next time you visit your favorite restaurant, you can proudly tell you friends that the restaurant operates in a monopolistic competitive market!

Chapter 2 Market Systems and Economies

Oligopoly

An **oligopoly market structure** has only a few sellers because it is very difficult to enter the market. Oligopolies can set their own price because they have control over part of the market. Examples of businesses in an oligopoly market structure include cars, steel, and oil. It takes a lot of work for a car company to become successful. Next time you ride a car to school, you should remember that the automobile industry operates in the oligopoly market structure.

Monopoly

In a **monopoly**, there is only one seller of a product. Wow! This makes the product very unique, allowing the monopoly to set their own price.

Examples of a monopoly include public utilities and first class mail. Your local cable television is another example of a monopoly. There is only one provider of cable television in your local area.

2.4 Types of Economies

There are four main economic systems: the market economy, the command economy, the traditional economy, and the mixed economy (the most common type).

Market Economy

In a **market economy**, goods and services are privately owned and a profit incentive exists. Refer to *1.2 Supply and Demand* for additional information.

Some characteristics of a market economy include:

- Private property rights
  - People have the right to own things like a house and a car with clear titles to their property.
- Competitive markets
  - Markets (supply and demand) determine the prices and quantities of goods and services.
- Voluntary exchange
  - An exchange of goods or services wouldn't take place unless buyers are willing to buy a certain product and sellers are willing to sell that product.
- Equilibrium Prices
  - Prices are determined by where supply intersects demand.
- Freedom of Choice
  - Individuals have the choice to decide what to do - whether they want to purchase something, live in a certain place, or have a certain job!
- Little government involvement
  - Individuals, rather than the government, decide what to produce, how to produce, and for whom to produce.

Command Economy

In a **command economy**, the production of goods and services is controlled by the government, rather than the interaction of supply of demand through the markets.

Some characteristics of a command economy include:
- The government makes decisions on economic activities.
- The government allocates resources.
- Low efficiency and little competition.
  - Since the government makes all of the choices, individuals have little incentive to work hard and businesses have little incentive to be efficient, because the profit motive is taken away due to government intervention.
- Low unemployment.
  - The government decides the wages and the number of jobs available, and therefore it can manipulate the unemployment rate and the distribution of wages.
- The government has the ability to deal with any externalities and inequality issues that may exist in the economy.

Chapter 2 Market Systems and Economies

Traditional Economy

In a **traditional economy**, the production of goods and services is operated based on past generations.

Characteristics of a traditional economy:
- Based on agriculture, hunting and gathering, and / or fishing.
- Little innovation.
  - Since the people who live in a traditional economy continue to follow old traditions, they have no reason to come up with new innovations.
- People could still use bartering, which is the trading of goods and services for other goods and services.

Mixed Economy

Since there is no country that strictly follows one type of economic system, the **mixed economy** is the most common type. Most countries, including the United States, contain characteristics from multiple types of economic systems.

Market + Command + Traditional = Mixed

Countries on the Economic Spectrum

TRADITIONAL ECONOMY

the Amish in Pennsylvania   Torres Strait Islanders

MARKET ECONOMY

the United States
South Korea   the United Kingdom

France   Mexico
India

Venezuela

China

Cuba

North Korea

COMMAND ECONOMY

Chapter 3: Money

- 3.1 Roles of Money
- Bananas: Why aren't they money?
- 3.2 Types of Money
- Diving a little Deeper...

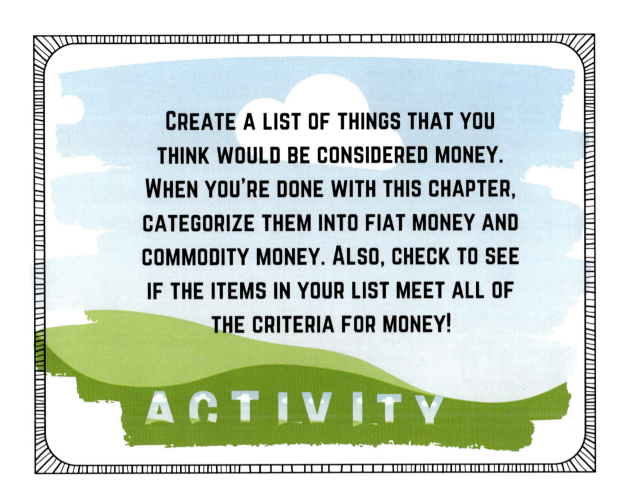

3.1 Roles of Money

What is considered money?

To be considered money, three requirements must be met: store of value, medium of exchange, and unit of account.

- **Store of value:** people can put money into their savings and retirement accounts with confidence that the value of the money will not be lost and will be retained over long periods of time. For example, you could put money in a piggy bank in hopes of saving up to buy something big! Therefore, the money acts as a store of value because it can be stored and spent at a later time without loss of value.

- **Medium of exchange:** all forms of money can be used as a form of transaction - the trade of goods and services between two different parties. In order for this condition to be met, the money must be commonly accepted as a form of payment. The most common medium of exchange today is currency, as everybody accepts it as a legal form of payment.

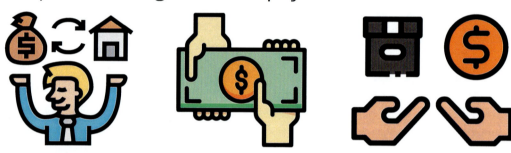

- **Unit of account:** money also serves as a unit of account, meaning that it can be used to assign values to different goods and services and to keep track of spending / payments. Money can easily be counted and used to show your earnings, debts, and wealth. For example, money acts as a unit of account when comparing the prices of two goods. In this case, the compared prices helps you understand different qualities of the goods and services, and can lead to better decision making. Additionally, when you receive an allowance, money allows you to see how much you have already spent, and how much you have left to spend!

Technically, anything that fits the three requirements of store of value, medium of exchange, and unit of account would be considered money. The most common money today is currency because it is widely accepted as a legal form of payment, it maintains value over time, and it assigns value to goods and services.

Let's go BANANAS for Economics! But why aren't bananas considered money?

Have you ever thought about using bananas as money?

First off, they do not meet the store of value requirement. Unlike saving coins in a piggy bank, bananas cannot be stored for a long time, and can rot very quickly. Bananas cannot be invested into savings or checking accounts, and cannot earn interest (unlike money).

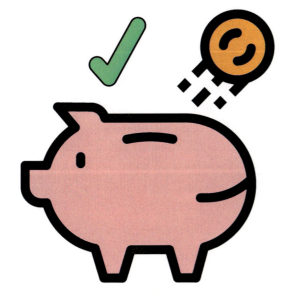 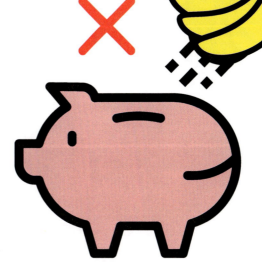

So, why don't things like bananas meet the medium of exchange requirement? Think about it - if you went to a garden and offered three bananas in exchange for a bouquet of flowers, it is very likely that the gardener will decline the offer.

In order to get a successful transaction...

- the gardener must actually want the three bananas and value them more than the bouquet of flowers that is being traded.
- If you encounter a gardener who wants apples instead, you would have to first go out and find apple farmers and see if any of them are interested in trading their apples for your three bananas.
- Then, you must go back and offer your apples in exchange for the bouquet of flowers from the gardener. As you can see, it is a very inefficient process!

Ok, so two of the three requirements are already out. What about a unit of account? Unfortunately, bananas do not meet this requirement either. You would never measure the prices of goods and services in bananas.

"Oh, this trampoline costs 5½ bananas, and the other one costs 7¾ bananas... I earned 8 bananas this month, and I owe ½ a banana..." Those scenarios would never happen! Since bananas do not meet any of the criteria, they are not considered money. Sorry, better not offer your bananas next time you go shopping!

Believe me, I've tried! It didn't go very well...

Chapter 3 Money

3.2 Types of Money

There are two types of money: fiat and commodity.

- **Fiat Money:** money that is issued and backed by the government, rather than by a commodity (see below). People accept this form of money because everyone else does, and is now the most common form of money throughout the world (including the United States).

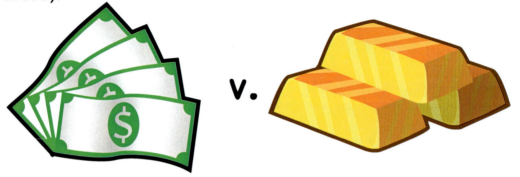

- **Commodity money:** money that derives its value from the object itself (commodity) from which it was made. Basically, an actual good itself would be used as money, and is thus backed by the value of the item itself. A historic example of commodity money is when money was backed by gold. Commodity money can often be extremely bulky, making it hard to use as a medium of exchange. There are other uses for commodity money - for example, gold can be used to create jewelry. Therefore, the value of the money came from the value of the gold itself, as opposed to fiat money (which is declared legal tender by the government, from which it gains its value).

Diving a little Deeper...

Let's have some fun!!!

Instructions: there will be a series of questions on the types of money along with its functions. Simply think about the corresponding answer choices and check to see if you are correct on the page to the right!

● ●

1. True or False: the Euro is fiat money

2. True or False: the US dollar is fiat money

3. True or False: silver is commodity money

4. Which one of the following is not a function of money?
    a. Store of Value
    b. Medium of Exchange
    c. To use as decoration
    d. Unit of account

ANSWER KEY

1. True; the Euro is an example of fiat money, because it obtains its value from the European Union, and since all of its member countries accept it as money and it is declared the legal form of money, it is an example of fiat money!

2. True; the US dollar is an example of fiat money, because it gets its value from the government. Since the US Dollar is widely accepted as a form of payment, this is what you spend when you go shopping with your parents!

3. True; silver is an example of commodity money, because it has other purposes outside of being used to exchange goods and services. Silver is commonly used for jewelry purposes. The value comes from the silver itself rather than from the government.

4. C; by process of elimination, we can see that the answer must be C, since the three functions of money are store of value, medium of exchange, and unit of account. For more refreshers of this, make sure to go back and review this chapter!

Digging a little Deeper...

Chapter 4: The US Economy

- 4.1 The Banking System
- 4.2 Fiscal Policy
- 4.3 Monetary Policy
- Fun Facts about the Fed

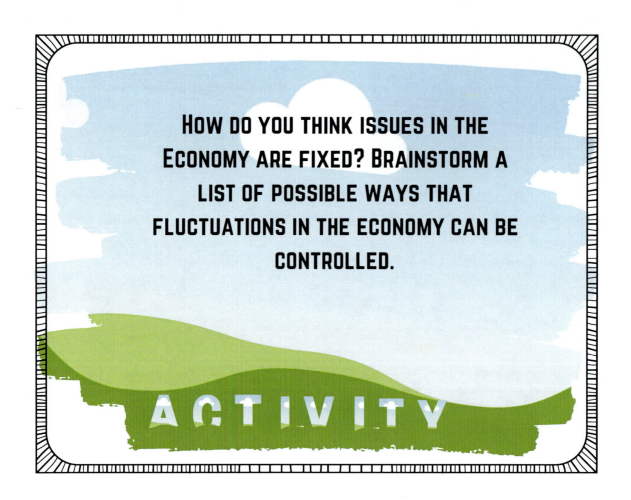

4.1 The Banking System

There were many financial crises in the early 20th century, including severe bank failures that led to an overall weak banking system.

Therefore, the **Federal Reserve**, more commonly known as the Fed, was established as the central bank of the United States in 1913. Ok, so you're probably thinking... "there are so many banks, what makes the Fed unique?" Great question! The Fed essentially controls the money supply of the United States, and has many different tools to do so. The main purpose of the Fed is to maintain the strength and stability of the banking system throughout the United States to avoid financial problems.

There are twelve Federal Reserve Districts, with the district banks (one for each district) located in major cities such as New York City, Atlanta, and Chicago.

4.2 Fiscal Policy

Fiscal policy is government's use of taxing and spending to help stabilize the economy. Unlike monetary policy, fiscal policy is directed and performed by the government instead of the Federal Reserve.

Depending on the situation in the economy, the government either employs expansionary fiscal policy (to expand the economy), or contractionary fiscal policy (to contract the economy).

- **Expansionary fiscal policy**: when the economy is not doing well, expansionary fiscal policy will be performed through an increase in government spending and a decrease in taxes.
    - This scenario would be represented on the PPC as a point inside the curve, since resources are not being used to their full potential. Since the economy is in a bad state, businesses are under-performing and prices are low. Therefore, the government will

stimulate activities in the economy by increasing their spending, which will lead to more consumer and business spending as well. Furthermore, taxes will be decreased, providing consumers with more money to spend, also leading to a stimulation of the economy.

- **Contractionary fiscal policy**: sometimes, the economy is over-performing, which can also lead to major consequences (overworked people, unsustainable development, etc).
  - This state would be represented on the PPC as a point outside of the curve, since the economy is producing more than they are capable of sustaining. To correct this problem, the government would decrease spending and increase taxes in order to slow down the unsustainable growth of the economy. With either fiscal policy tool, consumer and business spending will decrease, thus slowing down the economy as desired.

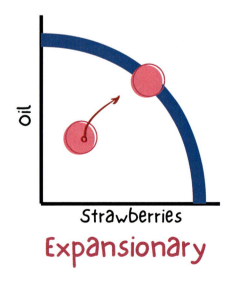

Expansionary

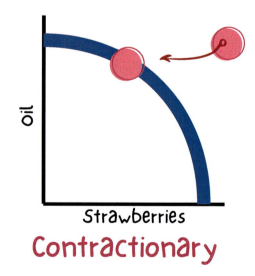

Contractionary

4.3 Monetary Policy

Monetary policy is performed by the central bank of the United States, the Federal Reserve. The main goals of monetary policy are to create maximum employment, long term economic growth, and stable prices. Monetary policy is all about controlling the money supply! There are three tools of monetary policy: open market operations, setting the discount rate, and changing reserve requirements.

- **Open market operations:** performing open market operations is the most common monetary policy tool utilized by the Fed. Open market operations refer to the buying and selling of bonds (essentially a contract between the two parties involved, in which one party lends money by buying the bond, and the other party owes money from selling the bond). When the Fed wants to increase the money supply (which would stimulate the economy), they would buy bonds, and if the Fed wants to decrease the money supply (which would slow down the economy), they would sell bonds.

- **Setting discount rate:** the discount rate is the interest rate (the payment on top of the original borrowed amount) that is set by the Federal Reserve. Other banks would then borrow funds from the Fed through the discount window. Therefore, if the discount rate increased, money supply would decrease (because banks would borrow less money, slowing down the economy), and if the discount rate decreased, money

Chapter 3 Money

supply would increase (because the banks would borrow more money - lower interest rates means that it is easier to return the money), stimulating the economy.

- **Changing reserve requirements:** reserve requirements are the amount of money that banks are required to hold from each deposit - this money cannot be lent out. Therefore, if the reserve requirement was increased, the money supply would decrease, because banks now have less money to loan out. This situation would slow down the economy due to having less money available to spend. On the other hand, if the reserve requirement decreased, money supply would increase, because banks now have more money to loan out, which would stimulate the economy due to increased borrowing and spending.

Contractionary   Expansionary

Sell Bonds	Buy Bonds
Increase discount rate	Decrease discount rate
Increase Reserve Requirements	Decrease Reserve Requirements

Fun Facts about the Fed

Missouri is the only state in the US that has 2 Federal Reserve district banks: one in Kansas City, the other in St. Louis.

The board of governors, consisting of 7 people, head the Federal Reserve. Every board member serves for 14 years.

THE FEDERAL RESERVE

Janet Yellen, who served as the Chair of the Federal Reserve from 2014 to 2018, was the first woman to lead the Fed.

The headquarters of the Fed are located at the Marriner S. Eccles Federal Reserve Board Building in Washington, DC.

Chapter 5: Gross Domestic Product

- 5.1 What is GDP?
- 5.2 Employment & Unemployment
- GDP Analysis

5.1 What is GDP?

Gross Domestic Product (GDP) is the total value of goods and services produced in a country during a set amount of time (usually one year).

The GDP is an important concept because it informs us about the performance of the economy.

Components of GDP

GDP = C + I + G + Xn. It seems pretty complex at first, but once you break it down, it becomes really simple!

- C stands for consumer spending.
  - As a consumer, you spend money on food, books, games, and more!

- I stands for investment.
  - Businesses need to make investments in order to grow. Your local bakery shop needs to invest in ovens and bread pans in order to produce more delicious baked goods for consumers to enjoy.

 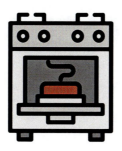 

Chapter 3 Gross Domestic Product

- G stands for government spending.

THINK OF YOUR FAVORITE PUBLIC PARK. DO YOU NEED TO PAY EVERY TIME YOU VISIT THE PARK? NO. THIS IS BECAUSE IT IS PAID FOR BY THE GOVERNMENT THROUGH COLLECTION OF TAXES. THIS IS ONE EXAMPLE OF GOVERNMENT SPENDING. NOW THINK OF YOUR LOCAL PUBLIC SCHOOL. DO YOU NEED TO PAY TO ATTEND? NO. EDUCATION IS A BIG PART OF LOCAL AND STATE GOVERNMENT SPENDING!

ACTIVITY

- Xn stands for net exports.
  - Net exports = exports - imports. Remember the last time you saw a sticker that said "Made in China"? That means the good was imported from China. But the U.S. also exports goods to other countries. For example, other countries buy U.S. exports of rice, cotton, wheat, and tobacco.

5.2 Employment & Unemployment

In the economy, workers are needed to produce goods and services. The **labor force** is the total number of people above the age of 16 who are qualified to work.

Unemployment occurs when people who want a job cannot get a job. There are three types of unemployment: cyclical, structural, and frictional.

- **Cyclical unemployment** is caused by the ups and downs of the economy and often results in workers being laid off.

- **Structural unemployment** happens when the workers do not have the skill set needed to complete a job. For example, workers were previously needed to assemble all the parts of a car. Today, those workers have been replaced by machines. But don't worry, those workers can get other jobs after further training.

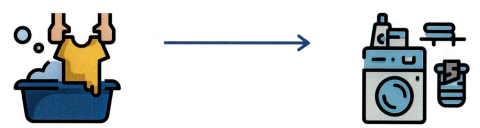

Chapter 5 Gross Domestic Product

- **Frictional unemployment** is caused by people transitioning between jobs. A college graduate who is looking for a job for the first time is an example of frictional unemployment.

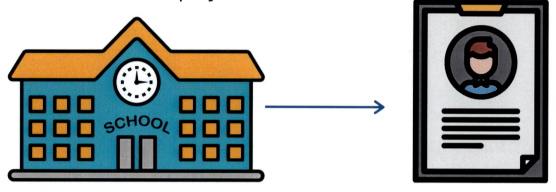

It is normal to have frictional and structural unemployment in our economy. Cyclical unemployment often requires more government intervention.

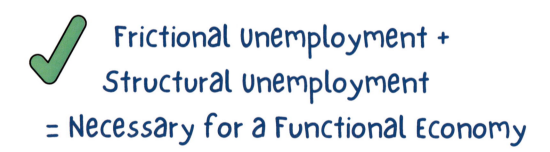

Frictional Unemployment +
Structural Unemployment
= Necessary for a Functional Economy

Cyclical Unemployment

GDP in a Nutshell

GROSS DOMESTIC PRODUCT:

the

MACROECONOMIC

We're looking at the big picture here!

Indicator

of the

Economy

Chapter 6: Basic Business Concepts

- 6.1 Business Organizations
- 6.2 Sole Proprietorships
- 6.3 Partnerships
- 6.4 Corporations
- Business Organizations Comparison

6.1 Business Organizations

There are three main types of business organizations: sole proprietorships, partnerships, and corporations. There are many advantages and disadvantages of each form of business organization. Let's explore more!

6.2 Sole Proprietorships

The **sole proprietorship** is the simplest form of business, where one person owns and operates the entire business. This is the most common type in the United States, however, it is not the type of organization that brings in the largest profit.

Advantages

- Relatively simple to start - there are very few documents required to begin a sole proprietorship.
- The owner has absolute control over his/her business - since there is only one owner, that owner keeps 100% of all the profits made. This way, there are no arguments between different owners (which is possible in other forms of businesses) since the owner makes all of the decisions.
- There are tax advantages - any profits that the business makes are counted as the income of the owner, and therefore those earnings would not be taxed two times (unlike a corporation), and therefore more of the money made can be kept by the owner.

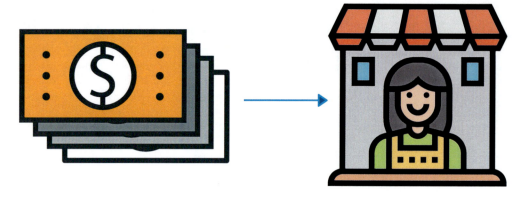

Disadvantages

- When the owner passes away, or decides to stop doing their business, the sole proprietorship ceases to exist.
- The owner has unlimited liability, meaning that their personal assets are at stake (including their house, car, etc). Unfortunately, while the owner keeps 100% of the profits, the owner also incurs 100% of the losses - that part doesn't sound as nice! Any debts of the business are therefore the debts of the owner.
- The owner has to do everything. There are many parts to managing and owning a business. Even if the owner is not skilled in some areas, he/she would have to learn, since he/she is the only person who is part of the business.

6.3 Partnerships

A **partnership** is more complex than a sole proprietorship, but less complicated than a corporation. In this form of business organization, two or more people form a business together.

Advantages

- More people to chip in means more resources! All of the partners can contribute resources to the business. As always, two or more heads are better than one, and therefore it can be significantly easier to come up with ideas and other business related needs.

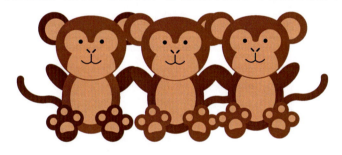 

- When there are two or more owners, the amount of work needed to be performed by each owner decreases, since partners will share the tasks. This way, owners will work in their skillful areas.
- Partnerships are also straightforward to set up, although not quite as simple as a sole proprietorship. Only a contract is needed, which makes it relatively easy to form a partnership.
- Earnings of the businesses are filed as the income of the owners. Therefore, the same money is not taxed twice.

Chapter 6 Basic Business Concepts

Disadvantages

- All of the owners have unlimited liability, meaning that their personal assets are at stake (including their house, car, etc). Unfortunately, while the owners split the profits, the owners must also split the losses, meaning that the partners can be responsible for the unprofitable actions of other partners! Any debts of the business are the debts of the partners.

- The success of a partnership ultimately relies on the partnership contract! If little effort was put into the contract, or if it was poorly written, many problems could come into play later on. For example, if one partner wants to leave, but the contract didn't specifically say how to do so, problems could arise.

6.4 Corporations

Corporations are the most complex of all business organizations, but they also bring in the largest amount of money. A **corporation** has many owners, and it can easily accumulate resources.

Advantages

- All of the owners have limited liability! This means that the personal assets of the owners are not at risk.
- Corporations do not end when owners leave - they will continue to exist as long as the current owners wish for them to continue.
- Believe it or not, it is extremely easy to have new owners! Ownership in a corporation simply means that you invested money into the company by purchasing stock. A company's stockholders will receive a portion of the profits that the company earns. Stocks are easily transferable, leading to frequent changes in ownership.

- Corporations can raise money quickly, providing them with the ability to grow and become competitive.

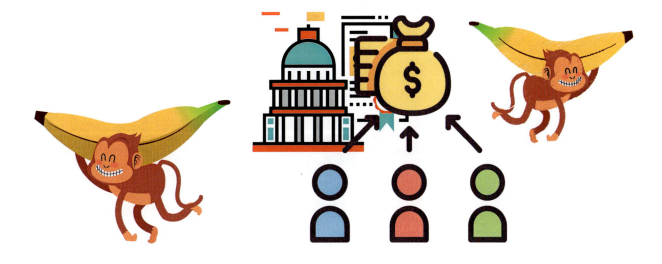

Chapter 6 Basic Business Concepts

Disadvantages

- Corporations can be very complicated and difficult to establish. The requirements for corporations are set high, leading to possible high costs to meet those requirements.

- Corporations are regulated by the government. Corporations must meet all of the requirements set by the government in order to eliminate possible penalties and fines.

- Any profits that the corporation earn are taxed and then the income that is passed on to the owners (through stocks) is taxed again. Therefore, the profits earned are taxed twice.

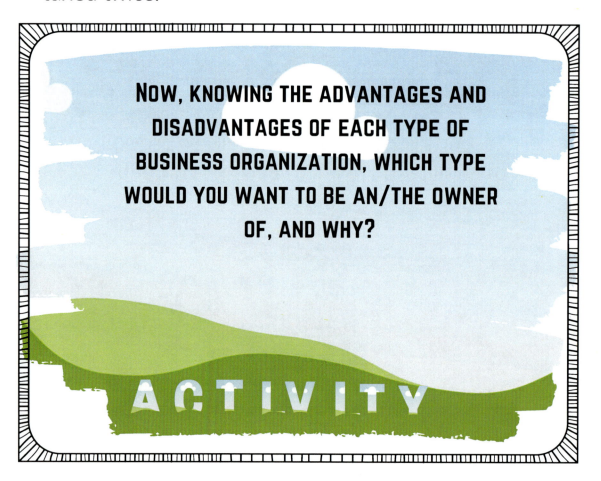

NOW, KNOWING THE ADVANTAGES AND DISADVANTAGES OF EACH TYPE OF BUSINESS ORGANIZATION, WHICH TYPE WOULD YOU WANT TO BE AN/THE OWNER OF, AND WHY?

ACTIVITY

Business Organizations Comparison

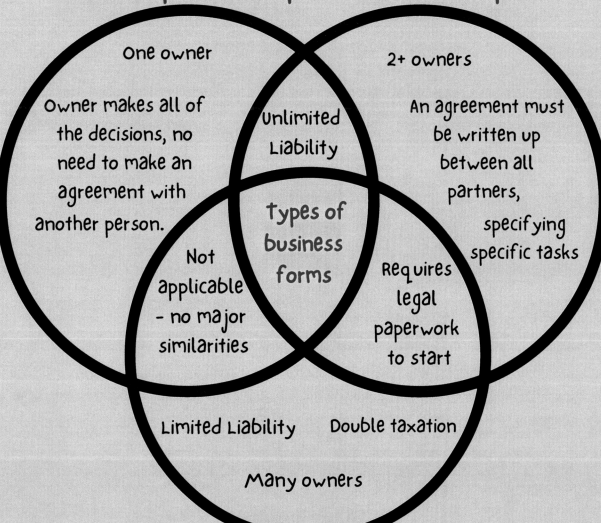

Sole Proprietorship

One owner

Owner makes all of the decisions, no need to make an agreement with another person.

Partnership

2+ owners

An agreement must be written up between all partners, specifying specific tasks

Unlimited Liability

Types of business forms

Not applicable - no major similarities

Requires legal paperwork to start

Limited Liability

Double taxation

Many owners

Corporation

Chapter 7: International Trade

- 7.1 Where do our everyday objects come from?
- The reasoning behind International Trade

7.1 Where do our everyday objects come from?

ON A SHEET OF PAPER, DRAW YOUR FAVORITE COTTON T-SHIRT!

ACTIVITY

Let's chat about where your t-shirt came from!

- First, the cotton was picked from a cotton field in Texas.
- Then, the cotton was shipped to a textile mill in China / India to be made into yarn.
- The yarn is then shipped to Bangladesh to be sewn.
- Finally, the sewn cloth can be shipped to retail stores all around the world.

Chapter 7 International Trade

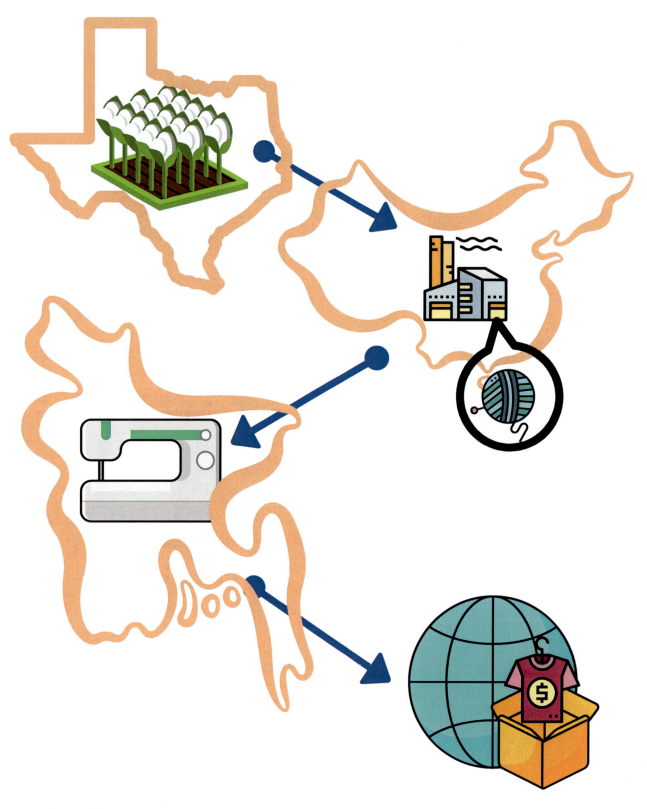

This demonstrates the idea of international trade - countries all specialize in a certain task and trade with each other. Now you know where your cotton t-shirt came from!

The reasoning behind International Trade

Countries trade to become more

EFFICIENT

and to

purchase foreign goods & services
that are

CHEAPER

than the ones in their own
country.

GLOSSARY

Capital
One of the factors of production that can be used to produce goods and services

Changing reserve requirements
The Federal Reserve increases the reserve requirement to decrease the money supply and decreases the reserve requirement to increase the money supply

Command economy
A type of economy where the government controls the production of goods and services

Commodity money
Money that derives its value from the object (commodity) from which it was made

Contractionary fiscal policy
When the government decreases government spending or increases taxes

Corporation
A company that acts as a legal entity

Cyclical unemployment
A type of unemployment that is caused by ups and downs in the business cycle

Demand
Demand is created when a consumer is able and willing to buy a certain good at set prices

Entrepreneurship
When a person takes risks and combines the three factors of production to produce goods and services

Equilibrium point
The point where supply and demand intersect

Expansionary fiscal policy
When the government increases government spending or decreases taxes

Federal reserve
The central bank of the United States

Fiat money
Money that derives its value from being declared legal tender by the government

Fiscal policy
When the government adjusts taxes and government spending to stabilize the economy

Frictional unemployment
Unemployment caused by people transitioning between jobs

Gross domestic product (GDP)
The total value of goods and services produced in a country during one year

Labor
A factor of production that includes the workers that are needed to produce goods and services

Labor force
The total number of people above the age of 16 who are qualified to work

Land
A factor of production that includes all natural resources such as water, trees, and soil

Limited resource
A resource that is finite and is often used at a faster rate than it is replenished

Marginal analysis
Examining the additional net benefit from consuming another unit of a good or service

Market
A place where items are exchanged

Market economy
A type of economy where goods and services are privately owned and a profit incentive exists

Medium of exchange
A function of money that allows it to be used as a form of transaction

Mixed economy
An economy that contains different characteristics from multiple types of economies

Monetary policy
A policy used by the Federal Reserve that involves controlling the money supply

Monopolistic competitive market
An economic system where there are many businesses that sell differentiated products

Monopoly
A market structure where there is only one seller of a unique product

Oligopoly market structure
A market structure where a few firms have most of the sales in the industry

Open market operations
A monetary policy tool that refers to the buying and selling of bonds

Overutilization
The situation where resources are used to their limit.

Partnership
A form of business organization where two or more people form a business together

Perfectly competitive market
A market structure where many businesses sell the same product at the market price

Production possibilities curve
A model that shows the different combinations of two goods that can be produced given current resources and technology

Quantity demanded
The amount of a good or service that the consumer is willing and able to purchase at a certain price

Quantity supplied
The amount of a good or service that the producer is willing and able to sell at a certain price

Setting discount rate
The interest rate the Federal Reserve charges financial institutions for loans

Sole proprietorship
A business organization where one person owns and operates the entire business

Store of value

A function of money that allows it to maintain purchasing power over time

Structural unemployment

A type of unemployment that occurs when workers do not have the skill set needed to complete a job

Supply

the amount of a good or service that producers are willing and able to sell at set prices, ceteris paribus

trade-offs

When consuming more of one good or service means consuming less of another good or service

Traditional economy

An economic system where the production of goods and services is based on the past generations

Underutilization

When the factors of production are not being used efficiently and production is at a point inside of the Production Possibilities Curve

Unemployment

When people in the labor force are looking for a job but cannot get one

Unit of account

A function of money that allows it to be used to assign value to different goods and services

About the authors

Janet Liu & Melinda Liu both have a strong passion for economics. They are the founders of the 501(c)(3) nonprofit Sunrizon Economics, creators of the Wonderland Economics YouTube channel and the MyEconda e-learning platform, and the authors of *Elementary Economics; A True Book: Making and Saving Money;* and *Making and Saving Money: Jobs, Taxes, Inflation... And Much More!*

They hope to share their love for economics with more students, helping them develop their understanding of economics from a young age.

Though they initially wrote this book in high school, Janet and Melinda are now studying Computer Science and Economics at MIT.

Made in United States
North Haven, CT
21 April 2025

68155453R00035